FEAR NOT

By: Malcolm Smith

Study Guide

INSTRUCTIONS

Welcome to **Fear Not** by Malcolm Smith – your guide to conquering fear and anxiety through the unconditional love of God.

This Study Guide is a supplement to Malcolm Smith's **Fear Not** video series for small group studies. Use this workbook to take notes and journal your thoughts as you watch each session of the Fear Not series. Fill in the blanks as you learn and take opportunities to pause the video as needed to discuss each concept with your group.

Each session concludes with a set of Reflection Questions which you can use as a starting point for conversation in your group, and for exploring each concept as it applies to your life and situation.

FEAR NOT

INTRODUCTION

Session 1

In These Sessions:

We will be **sharing the** that **Jesus Christ brings us out** of the **anxiety** and that have a tyrannical hold over us

I have known **Raised in London during WW2** living my first years of life in **bomb shelters** watching the

faces of the adults

what
is, and **its**
cause

God is
relentless,
                    LOVE
to **Save Us** from our
Core

THE LIE...

that God
himself from us and became an
        and   **god**

Session #1 "Introduction"

But God...

Joined Himself to us in ___ and
destroyed the ___ coming
to dwell within us through the ___

He is in us – in **every** detail of life

His presence is the end
of ___ and **anxiety**

Isaiah 41:10 (NKJV)

___ **not**, for I am with you;
Be not dismayed, for I am your God.
I will ___ you,
Yes, I will help you,
I will uphold you with My righteous right hand.

Reflection Questions:

What is your greatest **FEAR**?

How have you **coped** with your **FEAR** and **Anxiety**?

What do you **hope** to get from this study?

the TWO KINDS of FEAR

Session 2

FEAR placed in us by the creator to activate all our physical systems when faced with real danger; it **releases** into the body propelling us into action –

either **or** .

There are **real, rational** and **normal fears** that make up a   human.

FEAR-FULLNESS:

- Was **NOT**   by the **Creator** but the **Satanic**   of the original design.

- Describes living in a   **of FEAR** and   , life in the dimension of the   and **fantasy**

FEAR rises from the within our core, confusion to our entire system and brings
into our physical organs

Producing **and pain** – so powerful that fear causes shaking of the body!

Joshua 2:11 (NIV)

When we heard of it, our **hearts** ▢ **in fear** and everyone's failed because of you, for the LORD your God is God in heaven above and on the earth below.

Ways Fear Destroys The Human Body:

- Leads To A **Weakened**   System
- Impairs   Memory
- Interrupts Processes To   Emotions
- Is The   To Love's Intention
- Establishes **Suspicion &**
-          The **Peace** & Joy
- Is   **For** Worry, Anxiety, Distress, Panic & Terror

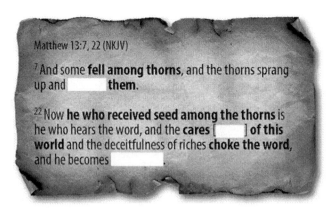

wor·ry /ˈwərē/ *verb*

1. From an old word meaning to **shake by the neck, to** ,
   and ;

   See also: **distress, terror, panic;**

Matthew 13:7, 22 (NKJV)

7 And some **fell among thorns**, and the thorns sprang up and _____ **them**.

22 Now **he who received seed among the thorns** is he who hears the word, and the **cares [_____] of this world** and the deceitfulness of riches **choke the word**, and he becomes _____.

Distress:

Describes a _____ **place**,
a canyon too narrow to turn around;
feelings of

imprisonment, **overwhelmed** and
constrained by circumstances

Terror:

Expecting   and **destruction** behind every corner and in every situation.

The sense of   **hiding** in every public place.

Panic:

The sense of every fear leaping upon **from every side** to   the mind and send the emotions into   .

Religious Anxiety:

Living under an image of a   that is against us, **condemning** and producing in us guilt, shame and despair of **never being**   or accepted.

11

Reflection Questions:

How much of your life is **limited by fear**?

What **steps can you take** to change?

Isaiah 41:10 (NKJV)

_____, for I am with you;
Be not dismayed, for I am ____ God.
I will strengthen you,
Yes, I will ____ you,
I will uphold you with My righteous right hand.

The Greatest Questions We Can Ask:

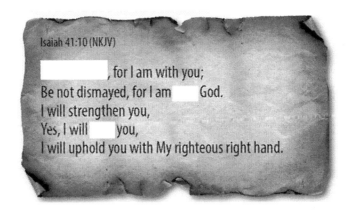

Who is the _____ of the _____
promise?

Who is **He whose
presence** with us _____
the fear?

13

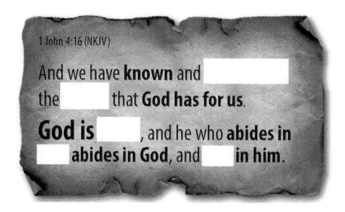

1 John 4:16 (NKJV)

And we have **known** and [____] the [____] that **God has for us**.
God is [____], and he who **abides in** [____] abides in God, and [____] in him.

God is Love:

He does not merely [____] **love**
- He [____] love
- Love is **His** [____]

He [____] **His love, we do** not **call it into being**

God is Love:

He cannot be [____]
or [____]

Love is **unique to Him** – [____]

Definition of Agape:

He is **limitlessly**   **-for-**
relentlessly **seeking the highest** and
for the other

He is **unrelenting**
moving to **embrace** and   with the other

Definition of Agape:

He is set in His will to **overcome** all
that would   from **His**   **of**
union

He passionately desires to **unconditionally**
accept and   in the other

Definition of Agape:

The **passionate intention**
of God is to hold you in arms of

delighting in you

Zephaniah 3:17 (NKJV)

The LORD your God in your midst,
The Mighty One, **will save**;
He will _____ **over you** with gladness,
He will **quiet you** with His love,
He will _____ **over you with singing**."

Reflection Questions:

If this **God who is love** is with me, how is it
possible to fear?

Have you ever **stood in awe** and **wonder** at the
love of God for you?

16

God is love:

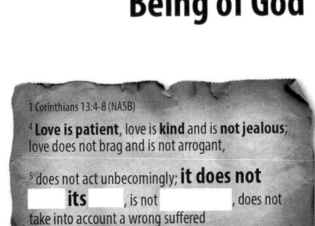

demands
that there must be
more than **one**
in the
Being of God

1 Corinthians 13:4-8 (NASB)

⁴ **Love is patient**, love is **kind** and is **not jealous**; love does not brag and is not arrogant,

⁵ does not act unbecomingly; **it does not** _____ **its** _____, is not _____, does not take into account a wrong suffered

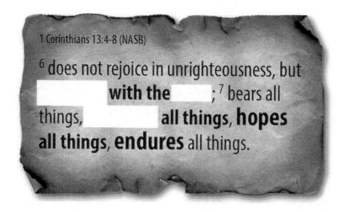

1 Corinthians 13:4-8 (NASB)

⁶ does not rejoice in unrighteousness, but _____ **with the** _____ ; ⁷ bears all things, _____ **all things, hopes all things, endures** all things.

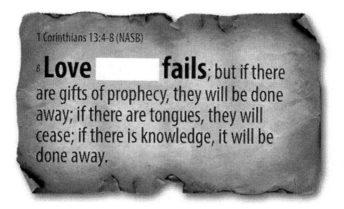

1 Corinthians 13:4-8 (NASB)

⁸ **Love** _____ **fails**; but if there are gifts of prophecy, they will be done away; if there are tongues, they will cease; if there is knowledge, it will be done away.

God is love: **The** _____ is not **weird** but the **revelation** of the unearthly **Love of God**

The Three are _____ in limitless agape so intense that the **Three are One** described as being each " " the other.

The Lover; the Beloved; the Love, the Fellowship:

The incredible   from
before creation was that the
triune God of love
willed to   with us
humans

The Lover; the Beloved; the Love, the Fellowship:

That you and I should be **elevated**

by the sheer   **of God** to

be   within the circle of

divine love

The Lover; the Beloved; the Love, the Fellowship:

to **partake** and

in the

of the **Father, Son & Holy Spirit**

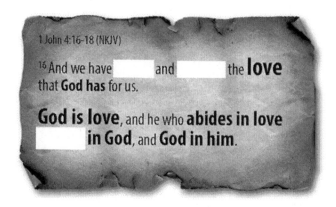

1 John 4:16-18 (NKJV)

16 And we have ____ and ____ the **love** that **God has** for us.

God is love, and he who **abides in love** ____ **in God**, and **God in him**.

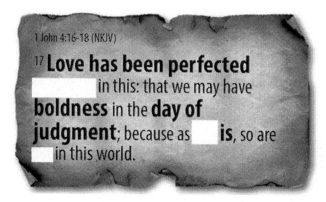

1 John 4:16-18 (NKJV)

17 **Love has been perfected** ____ in this: that we may have **boldness** in the **day of judgment**; because as ____ **is**, so are ____ in this world.

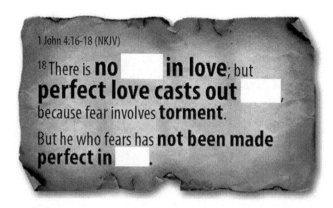

1 John 4:16-18 (NKJV)

18 There is **no** ____ **in love**; but **perfect love casts out** ____ because fear involves **torment**. But he who fears has **not been made perfect in** ____.

Fear is the
to focus on
and in the
love of God

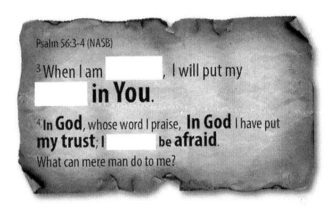

Psalm 56:3-4 (NASB)

³ When I am ⬚, I will put my ⬚ **in You**.

⁴ **In God**, whose word I praise, **In God** I have put **my trust**; I ⬚ be **afraid**. What can mere man do to me?

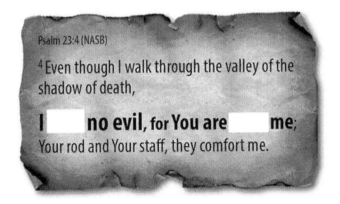

Psalm 23:4 (NASB)

⁴ Even though I walk through the valley of the shadow of death,

I ⬚ **no evil, for You are** ⬚ **me;** Your rod and Your staff, they comfort me.

Session #4 "The Circle of Love"

Do you **see yourself** as **residing** in the **heart** of the **Holy Trinity?**

How does that **change** your daily life?

Do you believe there are things about you that make it **impossible** for **God to love you?**

If being at home in the **of God** was the original blueprint, **what on earth happened** to land us in the broken mess and   that we find ourselves in today?

Where do our FEARS come from?

Into the paradise of **Eden**, came _____ in the form of a serpent to bring the first humans a **life changing message of the** _____.

Satan is the _____ and can only speak lies his only relationship to truth is to _____ **it** **and distort it**

Satan Is:

The **Liar**
The _____
The _____ **-Bringer**
The **Thief**
The **Destroyer**

24

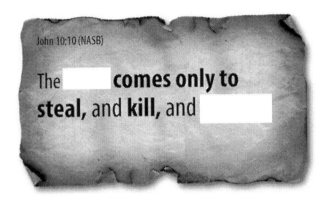

John 10:10 (NASB)

The ⬚ comes only to steal, and kill, and ⬚

John 8:44-45 (NASB)

You are of your **father the devil**, and you want to do the **desires** of your father.

He was a murderer from the beginning, and does not stand in the truth, because **there is no** ⬚ **in him.**

Whenever he **speaks a lie**, he speaks from his own ⬚; for he is a liar, and the ⬚ **of lies.**

Genesis 3:4-5 (NASB)

And the serpent said to the woman, **"You surely shall not** ⬚**!**

For God knows that in the day you eat from it your eyes will be opened, and **you will be like** ⬚, knowing good and evil."

They did not become gods, instead they were born again into a **darkness**, and **emptiness** they had never known existed

Adam no longer stood in wonder awe and delight at the passionate **love** in the **of God** but in of an imaginary **false judge deity** eager to punish

What happened in Eden was and is **deeper than breaking** .

The **love** between God and man was **shattered**

In the gap of
was **FEAR**
with its tormenting
anxiety and

The Liar & The Thief:

the **Face of God**

Stealing our **Core**

The **Illusion of**

Man's first words: **"I Was**   **"**

We have **defined man** the Fall of
mankind in terms of **Bad**

but it is more like a   that
plunged the human race into the
bottomless pit of

God in _____ has come into our core
of anxiety _____ **condemnation** or
judgment

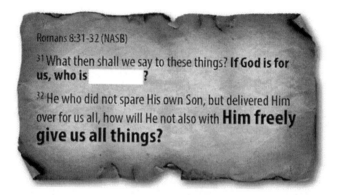

Romans 8:31-32 (NASB)

[31] What then shall we say to these things? **If God is for us, who is** _____ ?

[32] He who did not spare His own Son, but delivered Him over for us all, how will He not also with **Him freely give us all things?**

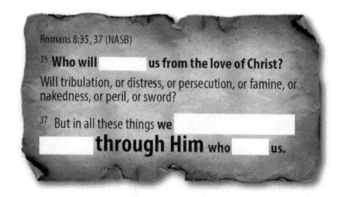

Romans 8:35, 37 (NASB)

[35] **Who will** _____ **us from the love of Christ?** Will tribulation, or distress, or persecution, or famine, or nakedness, or peril, or sword?

[37] But in all these things we _____ _____ **through Him** who _____ us.

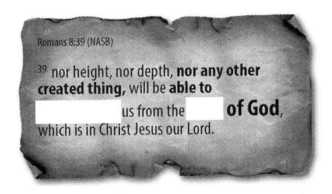

Romans 8:39 (NASB)

39 nor height, nor depth, **nor any other created thing,** will be **able to** _____ us from the ___ **of God,** which is in Christ Jesus our Lord.

Reflection Questions:

How does anxiety **interfere with your relationship** to God?

Do you feel **separated** from God?

Do you feel that **He does not care?**

Session 6

Love's
Amazing
Plan

The Lie
Changed Adam

He **could not**   the voice of love
only a god of judgment and rejection

He **believed he was**   in a hostile world
and could not hear anything that **contradicted** that

He was **unable to reach out to God** – he did not know
who that God was and **did not**   in a welcome

30

Immanuel (God _____ Us)

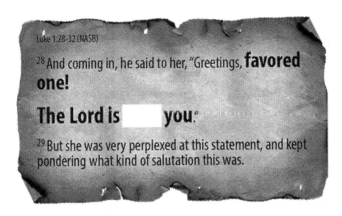

Luke 1:28-32 (NASB)

²⁸ And coming in, he said to her, "Greetings, **favored one!**

The Lord is _____ **you."**

²⁹ But she was very perplexed at this statement, and kept pondering what kind of salutation this was.

Luke 1:28-32 (NASB)

³⁰ The angel said to her, "**Do not be** _____, Mary; for you have **found** _____ **with God**.

³¹ And behold, you will conceive in your womb and bear a son, and you shall name Him Jesus.

³² He will be great and will be called the **Son of the Most High**; and the Lord God will give Him the throne of His father David;

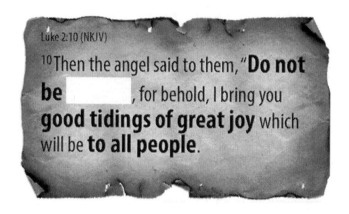

Luke 2:10 (NKJV)

¹⁰ Then the angel said to them, "**Do not be** _____, for behold, I bring you **good tidings of great joy** which will be **to all people**.

God In Our

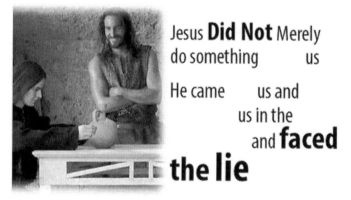

Jesus **Did Not** Merely do something _____ us

He came _____ us and _____ us in the _____ and **faced** _____ **the lie**

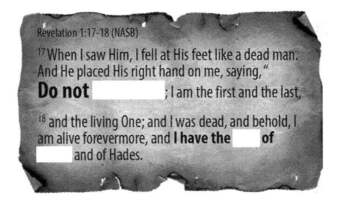

Revelation 1:17-18 (NASB)

[17] When I saw Him, I fell at His feet like a dead man. And He placed His right hand on me, saying, " **Do not** _____ ; I am the first and the last,

[18] and the living One; and I was dead, and behold, I am alive forevermore, and **I have the** ____ **of** ____ and of Hades.

No Separation
– the end of

Have you thought of **salvation** as being **saved from fear**
and **anxiety** In this **present** moment?

Have you thought of **Christ's work** being "**as**" you or
merely "**for**" you?

How does this **change your attitude** to life?

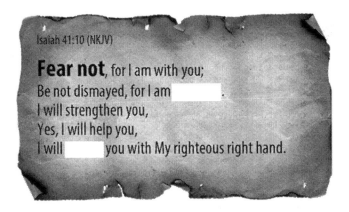

Isaiah 41:10 (NKJV)

Fear not, for I am with you;
Be not dismayed, for I am _____ .
I will strengthen you,
Yes, I will help you,
I will _____ you with My righteous right hand.

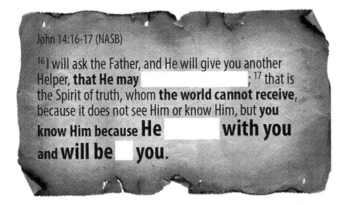

John 14:16-17 (NASB)

[16] I will ask the Father, and He will give you another Helper, **that He may** _____ ; [17] that is the Spirit of truth, whom **the world cannot receive**, because it does not see Him or know Him, but **you know Him because He** _____ **with you and will be** ___ **you.**

35

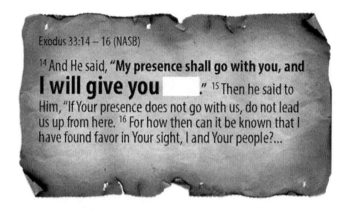

Exodus 33:14 – 16 (NASB)

¹⁴ And He said, **"My presence shall go with you, and I will give you _____."** ¹⁵ Then he said to Him, "If Your presence does not go with us, do not lead us up from here. ¹⁶ For how then can it be known that I have found favor in Your sight, I and Your people?...

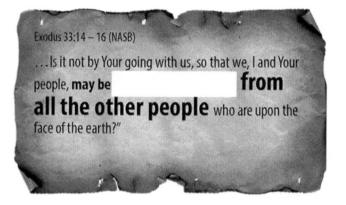

Exodus 33:14 – 16 (NASB)

...Is it not by Your going with us, so that we, I and Your people, **may be _____ from all the other people** who are upon the face of the earth?"

dis·tin·guished \dəˈstiNGgwiSHt/ *adjective*

1. _____; a wonder, a _____

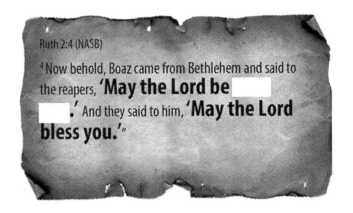

Ruth 2:4 (NASB)

⁴ Now behold, Boaz came from Bethlehem and said to the reapers, **'May the Lord be ___ ___.'** And they said to him, **'May the Lord bless you.'**"

The LORD Be With You:

Boaz greeted his workers with **"the Lord be with you"** and the response **"and the Lord bless you"**

They _____ oriented to the truth that **They Are Not**

It was not an empty "hello" but **A Continual** _____ of _____ And **Trust In God**

"The Lord" – "Be" – "With" – "You"

The Lord /thē lôrd/ *noun*

1. the translation of the Name of God, ___

2. the name of God who **entered into covenant** - the **giving of** ___ to them; **God giving** ___ delighting over and ___ **their lives**.

"The Lord" – "Be" – "With" – "You"

Be /bē/ *verb*

1. the **verb of** **, being,**

2. (*i.e.* **is** in this moment,   ) He **is** with you your companion step in your step whatever the moment holds – **He is now your love, wisdom, ability and meaning to the**

"The Lord" – "Be" – "With" – "You"

With /wĭth/ *preposition*

1. The triune God has **joined his life to** There is no situation you can find yourself in that he is not **walking** **and with you**

2. The   is swallowed up with **the truth that He is with us where we are Jesus changes this 'With' to an**

"The Lord" – "Be" – "With" – "You"

You /yo͞o/ *noun*

1. the   **individual that you are** with your unique abilities, fears and desires – He is **you** - as though you are the   one.

Reflection Questions:

Do you feel **alone and struggling** to make sense of life?

How has the **Holy Spirit revealed** to you that you are never alone?

the AMAZING "IS MY"...

Session 8

Isaiah 41:10 (NKJV)

Fear not, for I am ⬛ you;
Be not dismayed, for I am your God.
I will ⬛ you,
Yes, I will help you,
I will uphold you with My righteous right hand.

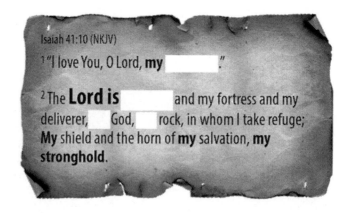

Isaiah 41:10 (NKJV)

[1] "I love You, O Lord, **my** ⬛."

[2] The **Lord is** ⬛ and my fortress and my
deliverer, ⬛ God, ⬛ rock, in whom I take refuge;
My shield and the horn of **my** salvation, **my**
stronghold.

When **anxiety** is triggered and   , step into the truth

Faith in that moment Announces:

"The LORD is   ..."

The LORD Is My:

The Lord: the   of God's love, strength, wisdom and ability

Is: in this   bringing new possibilities

My: all that God is has been   for my weakness and confusion; we can call all God is as   !

The LORD Is My:

We **Fill in the**   depending on the **problem** or need

Go through the Psalms and see the multiple times that **David**   **in the**   ...

The Lord was in him **everything the**   **demanded**

Reflection Questions:

In a **moment of anxiety**, how do we
step into the truth that He is with us?

Can you see in **Psalm 27** how **David**
applied this **truth?**

ANXIETY *and* IMAGINATION

Session 9

Isaiah 41:10 (NKJV)

Fear not, for I am ⬚;
Be not dismayed, for I am ⬚.
I will strengthen you,
Yes, I will help you,
I will uphold you with My righteous right hand.

Imagination /i͵majə'nāSH(ə)n/ *noun*

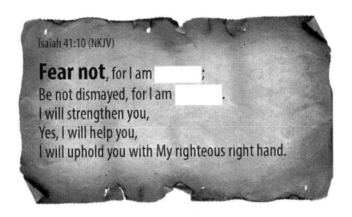

- **To** ⬚ ;
- **The** ⬚ **Place**, to see & ⬚ with the **invisible**
- **Develop a** ⬚

IMAGINATION in the Bible:

The Scripture uses many words to translate this fact into English:

- "   " or "combining"
- "   "
- "to plot,   , devise"
- "mind" or "   "

IMAGINATION:

- Is **Not**

- **God**   and marks us out as **different** to all other **creatures**

- Is our **inner**

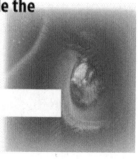

IMAGINATION:

- The ability to **Step Outside the Present**

- To   Beyond **Present Limitations**

- Is the **Place of**

Genesis 11:6-7 (NASB)

... this is what they began to do, and now nothing which they _____ (*imagine*) to do will **be** _____ for them.

The **imagination was** _____ by the **Accuser** in the garden to become a place of **imaging** _____ and fantasy out from the blinded self-for-self; **it is the soil in which all** _____ **grow**

His words were **directed** to the _____
— words **imaging** what they had **never thought**
— **becoming**

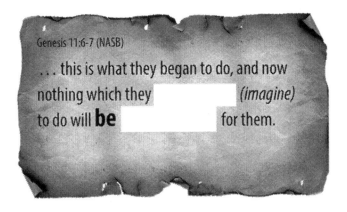

The fruit of the tree looked like a **piece of fruit** but **imagination** saw it as a **doorway to** _____

Genesis 3:6-7 (NASB)

...when the woman _____ that the **tree was good** for food, and that it was a **delight** to the eyes, and that the **tree was** _____ to make one wise, she took from its fruit and ate; and she **gave also to her husband with her**, and he ate.

Terrifying Time Travel:

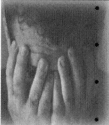

- Can make us relive and ____ the pain of the ____
- We come under the ____ of the ____ of that past moment
- We ask "What if... " and immediately step into a ____ that *is*
- *We experience shame of* "*I am* ____"

IMAGINATION:

The body ____ it as actually happening releasing the chemical into our body producing the **flight, fight** or **freeze** experience

Even though the event **is** ____ and ____ probably ____ **happen**

Faith:

All **faith includes** ____ in which we picture the ____ of the Lord being with us;

We see with **eyes of the** ____ our inclusion into Christ and the Spirit ____ with us in the ____ **moment**

IMAGINATION:

We _____ our painful résumé, a disastrous future

or

_____ at God's past, present and **future salvation**

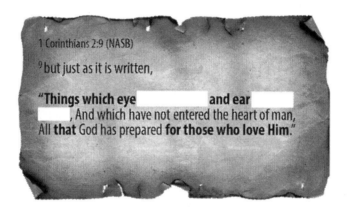

1 Corinthians 2:9 (NASB)

⁹but just as it is written,

"Things which eye _____ **and ear** _____, And which have not entered the heart of man, All **that** God has prepared **for those who love Him."**

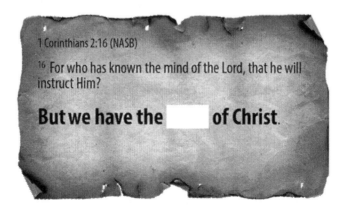

1 Corinthians 2:16 (NASB)

¹⁶ For who has known the mind of the Lord, that he will instruct Him?

But we have the _____ **of Christ**.

Session #9 "Anxiety and Imagination"

Reflection Questions:

Do you see the **Spirit in David's imagination**
in **Psalm 23**?

How does the **Lord fit** into **how you imagine**
your day, work, family?

REVIEW

Session 10

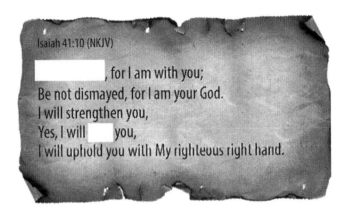

Isaiah 41:10 (NKJV)

_____, for I am with you;
Be not dismayed, for I am your God.
I will strengthen you,
Yes, I will _____ you,
I will uphold you with My righteous right hand.

I have known
Raised in London
during living
my first years of life in
bomb shelters
watching the
terrified
faces of the adults

The fact that **God is**

He does not merely

but **His Being**

is

The fact that **God**

He **does not**   in

to our behavior

It is **His love** that **changes**
our **behavior**

The fact that the **sin
of Adam** was not
breaking
and coming under
condemnation
and

It was **breaking** **with God** **of love** and entering the **Satanic** that we are now **from God**.

All our **anxiety** **takes place in the** of that **separation**

Terrifying Time Travel:

- Can make us **relive** and **re-feel the pain of the past**
- We come **under the control** of the anxiety of that past moment
- We ask **"What if..."** and immediately step into a future that *is Not*
- We experience shame of *"I am not"*

Jesus is **God**   **to**
us and **forever**
destroying the   of a
remote disinterested false god;

He is God **coming where**
        to **bring**   to
where He is

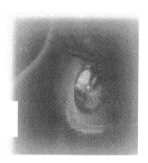

The **Spirit**
dwells **in Us**
He has **joined**
our

Reflection Questions:

How has **God's Love Changed** your Life?

Has the **Lord** entered your **imagination**?

How has this study **impacted** your **FEAR**
and **anxiety**?